Life in Post-War Britain

Ple
'le
Re
Tex
spe
www

L3

Brian Williams

www.raintreepublishers.co.uk

Visit our website to find out more information about Raintree books.

To order:

☎ Phone 0845 6044371

🖷 Fax +44 (0) 1865 312263

🖃 Email myorders@raintreepublishers.co.uk

Customers from outside the UK please telephone +44 1865 312262

Raintree is an imprint of Capstone Global Library Limited, a company incorporated in England and Wales having its registered office at 7 Pilgrim Street, London, EC4V 6LB - Registered company number: 6695582

Edited by Kate de Villiers and Laura Knowles
Designed by Steve Mead and Debbie Oatley
Original illustrations © Capstone Global Library Limited 2010
Picture research by Mica Brancic and Elaine Willis
Production by Alison Parsons
Originated by Chroma Graphics (Overseas) Pte. Ltd
Printed and bound in China by Leo Paper Products Ltd

ISBN 978 0 431193 65 6 (hardback)
14 13 12 11 10
10 9 8 7 6 5 4 3 2 1

ISBN 978 0 431193 72 4 (paperback)
15 14 13 12 11 10
10 9 8 7 6 5 4 3 2 1

British Library Cataloguing in Publication Data
Williams, Brian, 1943-
Life in post-war Britain. -- (Unlocking history)
941'.085-dc22
A full catalogue record for this book is available from the British Library.

Acknowledgements
We would like to thank the following for permission to reproduce photographs: Advertising Archives pp. **10**, **12**; Alamy pp. **7** (Mirrorpix/© Trinity Mirror), **21** (© John James), **23** (© Andy Beckett), **24** (© Robert Harding Picture Library Ltd), **26** (© Epicscotland), **28** (© PE Forsberg); Corbis p. **25** (Richard Klune); Getty Images p. **5** (Harry Todd), **8** (Popperfoto/Bentley Archive), **9** (Reg Speller), **14** (Hulton Archive), **16** (Picture Post/Photo by Bert Hardy); Mary Evans Picture Library p. **18** (Classic Stock/H. Armstrong Roberts).

Cover photograph of children playing on a London Street reproduced with permission of TopFoto/Ken Russell.

We would like to thank Bill Marriott for his invaluable help in the preparation of this book.

Every effort has been made to contact copyright holders of material reproduced in this book. Any omissions will be rectified in subsequent printings if notice is given to the publishers.

All the Internet addresses (URLs) given in this book were valid at the time of going to press. However, due to the dynamic nature of the Internet, some addresses may have changed, or sites may have changed or ceased to exist since publication. While the author and Publishers regret any inconvenience this may cause readers, no responsibility for any such changes can be accepted by either the author or the Publishers.

Contents

Some words are shown in **bold**, like this. You can find out what they mean by looking in the glossary.

Changing times

In 1945, World War II ended. After six years of war, Britain was at peace. People were happy but knew many challenges lay ahead. After the war (post-war), each **decade** brought more changes.

In the 1940s, schools, homes, hospitals, and factories were rebuilt after war damage. In the 1950s, children were excited by jet planes and television. New **immigrants** arrived to settle in Britain. The 1960s brought cheaper foreign holidays, motorways, pop superstars, and saw American **astronauts** land on the Moon. In the 1970s, Britain changed its money and joined the **European Union**. The 1980s–2000s brought more changes, especially in everyday life: superstores, computers, mobile phones, and Internet shopping.

This book looks especially at how life changed for children. To unlock history, we can look at **evidence** from lots of **sources**, such as the census (see box below), books, diaries, newspapers, photographs, television and films, people's memories, and even toys. They all tell a story. Tables, graphs, and diagrams can make evidence easier to understand.

The census

The census is how the government finds out how many people live in the country. People fill in forms to answer questions, such as how many people live in each house, how old they are, and so on. A census has been held in Britain every 10 years since 1801. Most countries have censuses.

Every day adds a new page of history, and in new ways, such as Internet blogs. Your parents and grandparents lived through some of the history in this book. Ask them what they remember. Memories are an important part of history. One day it will be your turn to answer questions, such as "What was it like growing up in 2010?".

▲ This soldier is returning home from fighting in the war. The boy may not have been able to remember his father very well after so long away.

Rebuilding

Before World War II, Britain was a rich and strong country. It was the centre of the **British Empire**. Six years of war left Britain much poorer, even though it had been on the winning side.

The war caused terrible damage to many countries. In Britain, thousands of homes had been wrecked by bombs, leaving many families homeless. Areas where buildings had been destroyed by bombs were called bombsites. They became playgrounds for children. After 1945, there was much rebuilding, with **council houses** and **new towns**. Many families from the worst-hit parts of London and other cities were rehoused in new estates. Some moved into "prefabs" – small homes made, or prefabricated, in factories. Prefabs were meant to last 10 years, but many were still there 40 years later.

There were big changes to hospitals, schools, and industries. The National Health Service (set up in 1948) gave free medical care for everyone. The school leaving age was raised from 14 to 15. Coal mines, steel-works, and railways were nationalised, which meant they were taken over by the government. Times were hard. **Rationing** begun during the war did not end until 1954.

"If you want work that gives you every chance to get on – think about coal mining ... At 15, you earn 49/6 [about £2.50] above ground, 59/6 [£3] below ground."

National Coal Board advertisement

In the 1950s, coal mining offered a steady job. Does this advert (left) suggest that young people were less keen on becoming a miner?

Before and after World War II

In 1939:
- Britain ruled India
- Railways were private companies
- Children left school at 14
- Coal mines were private companies
- People paid the doctor

In 1949:
- India was independent
- Railways were state owned
- Children left school at 15
- Coal mines were state owned
- Going to the doctor was free

Not all the post-war changes lasted. The new towns and National Health Service are still here, but Britain's coal mines, steel-works, and railways are no longer run by the government.

▼ These children are playing on a bombsite, among houses ruined during the war.

New beginnings

In 1948, the ship *Empire Windrush* brought 492 **immigrants** from Jamaica. They had come as workers to help rebuild Britain. Britain had had a small black and Asian population for many years. Over the next 40 years, more newcomers came from the Caribbean, India, and Pakistan. Others arrived from Africa, Australia, China, Vietnam, and the **European Union**. Immigrants were often surprised by life in Britain. They brought a mix of cultures – new foods, music, religions, and languages.

Memories of *Windrush* arrivals
"When I came to England I lived in Brixton [London], near the market. I tell you, when I came here there were hardly any buildings standing …"

Lucile Harris came from Jamaica

People's memories help unlock history. Many West Indians had helped Britain during the war. Others were shocked to see the war damage when they arrived in Britain.

This photograph was taken in 1955, when these people had just arrived by ship into Plymouth from Jamaica.

"I first came to England with the RAF ... I came back in 1948 as the opportunity for jobs in this country was better than back home ..."

Clinton Edwards came from the Caribbean

▲ Britain's Comet airliner (1952) was the first jet to carry passengers.

In 1951, 8.5 million people visited the Festival of Britain in London. The event was meant to show off new ideas in arts and science. People admired the latest designs for everything from chairs to jet planes. Government minister Herbert Morrison called the Festival of Britain "a tonic for the nation". A tonic is something that makes you feel better. What do you think he meant?

Another exciting event was the **coronation** of Queen Elizabeth II in 1953. Many children had their first glimpse of "live" television, watching the new queen on small black and white screens. In 1947, there were only 35,000 television sets in Britain. By the end of 1953, there were 3 million. Today, there are 60 million – roughly one for every person!

Years of change

By the 1960s, more people could afford cars, washing machines, and holidays abroad. Young people had jobs and money to spend. They liked pop music, on **vinyl records** (1960s), then **cassettes** (1970s), and CDs (1980s). They shopped in "boutiques" for teenage fashions, such as jeans, boots, and mini-skirts. In the 1940s, most youngsters wore much the same styles of clothes as their parents. From the 1950s, each decade brought new youth fashions and crazes (see box below). Young people had more freedom, and often challenged old ideas.

This is a fashion photograph from a 1960s magazine. ▶

Crazes

Can you find out more about these crazes?
• hula hoops
• Teenage Mutant Ninja Turtles
• yo-yos
• Teletubbies
• Pokémon
• Action Man
• Barbie dolls
• skateboards
• Rubik's cubes

American singer Bob Dylan sang "the times they are a-changing". US **astronauts** walking on the Moon in 1969 was one sign of change. Another was the first email, sent in 1971. By the 1970s, computers were at work in shops and offices. The first computers in British schools in the early 1980s were BBC Acorn computers.

In 1971, British shoppers had new money, as the old pounds, shillings, and pence were replaced by the decimal coins we use today (100 pence = £1). In 1973, Britain joined the Common Market, now the **European Union**. Europe was replacing the **Commonwealth** as Britain's main trade partner. Some familiar things continued through the changes, such as children's television programme *Blue Peter* (first screened in 1958) and soap opera *Coronation Street* (1960).

Pop culture

In the 1960s and 1970s, the Beatles, Rolling Stones, and other bands made Britain a centre of "pop culture". One downside of these "swinging" times was the rise in the use of harmful drugs. Smoking cigarettes is much less common now, but drug misuse is still a serious health issue.

▲ This poster was used by the government to tell people about Britain's new money.

Home life

In the 1950s, on a cold winter's day, people put more coal on the fire. Few homes had central heating and double glazing. This soon changed, with DIY (do it yourself) stores opening. More people were also able to afford central heating and new windows, as well as washing machines and fridge-freezers for their kitchen. Bathrooms changed too, with people taking showers as well as baths. In the 1950s, not every home had a bathroom, or even an inside toilet.

De Luxe Model TMT-43, 4·3 cu. ft. "Family" Frigidaire.

◀ Advertisements such as this showed people how they could modernize their homes. "Gns" were guineas in old money. One guinea is roughly £1.05 in today's money, but it was worth a lot more.

NOW! THE **SIZE** YOU **NEED** IN THE **COLOUR** YOU **LIKE** FOR AS **LITTLE** AS **66** GNS!

This new 4.3 cu. ft. "Family" Frigidaire is ready to brighten your life with all the lively new colours you see here. Nothing smaller than this "Family" model is big enough. Big enough to hold all the food that should be kept fresh for the family, yet small enough to fit into any kitchen.

Match—and *glorify*—your kitchen colour scheme with a new Frigidaire in Snowy White, Cotswold Cream, Sherwood Green, Stratford Yellow, Olympic Red or Everest Blue! And remember,

Frigidaire's exclusive "Meter-Miser" power unit cuts operating costs to the bone—actually uses less current than an ordinary light bulb!

★ ★ ★

FREE! Write today (address below) for free illustrated literature that gives all the facts about Frigidaire and the exclusive "Meter-Miser" power unit (backed by 5-Year Warranty).

FRIGIDAIRE MODELS

TST-43 (standard 4·3 cu. ft.)	66 gns.
TMT-43 (de luxe 4·3 cu. ft.)	71 gns.
OMT-79 (standard 7·9 cu. ft.)	114 gns.
ODT-77 (de luxe 7·7 cu. ft.)	120 gns.
OMT-97 (standard 9·7 cu. ft.)	152 gns.
ODT-95 (de luxe 9·5 cu. ft.)	166 gns.

Prices include Purchase Tax and Delivery. See your Frigidaire Dealer or nearest large store about

Easier than ever HP Terms! from only £10.8.0 down and 24 monthly payments of 57/-

Also on view at all Electricity Board Service Centres.

FRIGIDAIRE

Regd. Trade Mark

MADE IN BRITAIN BY FRIGIDAIRE DIVISION OF GENERAL MOTORS LIMITED, STAG LANE, KINGSBURY, LONDON, N.W.9.

A chilly memory

"... we knew it was cold but not how cold. So in preparation, we had all our blankets made into mohair coats ... I was wearing my pyjamas, then a pair of trousers, then another pair of trousers, then a suit, then on top of that this thick, mohair blanket/coat. It was all itchy ..."

Mahmood Patel came to Britain from Barbados in 1961

Ask your parents or grandparents what they remember about what life was like when they were children.

Fifty years ago, hardly anyone in Britain ate burgers or pizza! Today, many people like "fast foods" and enjoy Italian, Chinese, Indian, Mexican, and Thai meals at restaurants. In the 1950s, there were no ready-meals in the supermarket. Most families ate home-cooked meals most days, with the occasional takeaway from fish and chip or pie shops.

There were also big changes in home entertainment (see page 22) and communication. In 1950, most homes had no phone – people used a pay-phone in a street phone box. Today, most children have their own mobile phone. People began using the Internet in the 1990s, and today more than half Britain's homes have **broadband**. In the 1950s, people wrote letters, but now email is far more common.

Game and gadget inventions timeline

1972 PONG arcade game

1978 Space Invaders arcade game

1985 Nintendo

1989 Nintendo Game Boy (handheld)

1996 Nintendo 64; Sony PlayStation

1997 Nokia Snake mobile phone game

2001 Microsoft Xbox

2004 Nintendo DS

2006 Sony PlayStation 3; Nintendo Wii

2007 Apple iPhone

Timelines can help to show how different things develop over time.

Jobs

In 1951, Britain had more than one million farm workers, and some farmers still used horses to pull ploughs. Today, there are far fewer farm workers and farmers use tractors and other machines.

In the 1950s, many people worked in local industries – making pottery in Stoke-on-Trent, bicycles in Nottingham, cars in Coventry, knives in Sheffield, ships on the River Clyde in Scotland, and steel at Port Talbot in South Wales. By the 2000s, many of these traditional industries had closed, or got much smaller. In the 1950s, Britain had 850 coal mines. Today, UK Coal runs just 13 coal mines.

▼ By the 1950s, fewer farmers were using horses. Most had bought tractors. This photograph shows a test to compare horses and tractors.

The value of money

In 1950, the average worker was paid just over £100 a year. In 2008, it was over £23,000. You could buy a lot more with £1 in 1950 than you can now.

As old industries shrank, new ones grew – such as leisure and travel, communications, and finance (banking) – at least until the financial problems that began in 2008. About 28 million people in Britain have paid jobs. The two biggest groups of workers are in government, health, and education (6.4 million workers) and in shops, hotels, and restaurants (6.1 million workers). Until the 1960s, some people did the same job for 30 or 40 years. That is unusual today. Now many workers change jobs or retrain to learn new skills several times in their working lives.

Jobs rise and fall

This table compares three industries in 1950 and 2000. See how the number of workers in each changed.

	1950	2000
Mining	841,000	9,000
Farming and fishing	1,100,000	538,000
Finance	489,000	5,151,000

Statistics help us to compare things and times.

In 1984, Britain's coal miners went on **strike**. It meant hard times for miners' families:

"I was 10 and living in Buxton [Derbyshire]. We collected money every Saturday on the marketplace to send to the families."

Sharon Rowe

Some events stay in people's memories. When told, they can help us imagine the past.

City and country

In the 1950s, most country towns and villages had bus services or trains to the nearest city. Now most people rely on cars. Many small railway lines were closed in the 1960s. Motorways were built to link big cities. Today, with more than 32 million vehicles on Britain's roads, traffic jams make many journeys slow.

Most people in Britain live in urban areas (cities and towns). In the 1950s–60s, many old city centres were rebuilt. Flats, office blocks, and shopping centres sprang up. Housing estates were built on the outskirts of towns and became known as suburbs.

▼ This photograph shows a grocer's shop in 1955. In what ways is it different to a supermarket today?

Which shop?

Where did people shop in the 1950s? Can you match these items with the shops where they were sold?

Item:

- cabbage
- radio
- trousers
- cod
- comic
- bread
- meat
- frying pan

Shop:

- fishmonger
- ironmonger
- baker
- electrical shop
- butcher
- newsagent
- greengrocer
- tailor

Imagine you could take a trip back in time to 1950. What would you notice? You might notice there were fewer cars, and more small shops in the high street. "The Co-op grocer came round selling fruit and veg from a horse and cart," remembers a man who grew up in Stockton-on-Tees in the 1950s. This was still a fairly common sight. In 1968, Britain got its first superstore, and today supermarkets are where we do much of our shopping. People can shop online, and the goods come by van, not by horse and cart.

A nation of "townies"

In England and Wales, nine out of ten people live in an urban area. In Scotland, it is seven out of ten. Britain's biggest urban areas have more than one million people. They are:

- West Midlands
- Greater Glasgow
- Greater Manchester
- West Yorkshire
- Greater London (more than 8 million people, by far the biggest).

Why do you think the five regions listed above have so many people?

Going to school

In class in the 1950s, children sat at desks. They wrote in exercise books with pencils or pens dipped in inkwells (small pots of ink). Sometimes they wrote with fountain pens. There were no rollerballs or fibretip pens.

Teachers' visual aids were film strips and photos. Children listened to schools radio, until television for schools started in 1957. They were interested in dinosaurs, but as they listened to *How Things Began*, a radio time-trip into prehistory, they had to use their imaginations – there were no pictures! Many children loved science and space travel. They listened to *Journey Into Space* on radio, and later watched science fiction films such as *It Came from Outer Space*, and programmes such as *Dr Who*, which started on BBC television in 1963.

In the 1980s, children used computers in school for the first time. ▶

Most children walked to school, cycled, or took a bus. Not many parents had cars to do a "school run". Children drank free school milk, and school dinner meant whatever the cooks dished up – no menu, no choices, and no vegetarian options.

Until the 1960s, almost all children sat the 11-plus exam to decide which secondary school they went to – a grammar school or a secondary modern. Since the 1960s, most children have gone to comprehensive schools. In 1972, the school leaving age was raised from 15 to 16.

Things school children were used to in the 1950s:

- no choice for school dinner

- short trousers for boys in junior school

- school uniform (caps for boys, hats for girls)

- writing "lines" if told off

- desk tops that shut on your fingers

- scratchy pens and ink blots

Higher education

In the 1960s, only 1 school-leaver in 20 (5 per cent) went to university. Today, the number is 1 in 3 (34 per cent). The figure is higher (45 per cent) in Scotland and Northern Ireland. In 1962, there were 31 universities in Britain; in 2008, there were more than 160.

Statistics, with percentages, show how things change. Why do you think there are more university students now than in the 1960s?

"I remember getting milk at school free, and putting it by the heater to defrost."

Yvonne Dorr,
Wardie School, Edinburgh

How things changed for women

In the 1950s, young women wanted more freedom. Advertisements promised an easier life at home, thanks to "labour-saving" aids such as washing machines and vacuum cleaners. Women also expected men to help more than they had before.

The women's movement of the 1960s–70s was about women wanting equal rights with men, especially at work. During World War II (1939–45), more than 6 million women had gone out to work. By 1950, most married women were once again housewives. A woman usually left her job if she got married. Only a small number of young women went to university.

Today, more than 12 million women are at work. Around 57 per cent of university students are female. The Christian Church has women priests, there are women pilots in the Royal Air Force (RAF), many women run businesses, and there are more women in Parliament. Yet some women are still often treated unfairly; women's pay is still often less than that of men in some jobs, for example.

Britain's first woman prime minister

Margaret Thatcher was the first woman to be British prime minister. She was born in 1925, in Grantham, Lincolnshire, and studied chemistry at university, before being elected a Member of Parliament (MP). She was prime minister from 1979 to 1990.

In the 1950s, most women's magazines were about cooking, clothes, and babies. By the 1970s, women's magazines also covered careers and politics. What do today's magazine racks tell you about women in the 21st century?

▲ These women students are at the University of Birmingham. Today more than half of Britain's university students are women.

Women in Parliament

Year	Number of women	Percentage
1951	17	2.7
1964	29	4.6
1987	41	6.3
1997	120	18.2
2005	128	19.8

This table shows there are more women in Parliament now than in 1951. However, the majority of MPs are men.

Entertainment

In 1948, London hosted the Olympic Games. There was little money to spend on stadiums and accommodation for the 4,000 competitors from 59 countries. The 2012 London Olympics will be much bigger, with more than 200 countries taking part – and will cost a lot more.

Many sports are now big business, with television companies paying a lot of money to screen games. Television changed home entertainment in Britain. In 1950, most families listened to the radio at home, and went out to the cinema perhaps once a week. Many children went to "Saturday morning pictures" at a local cinema. By the 1960s, most homes had a television set. In the 2000s, many homes have several televisions with lots of channels.

Britain's biggest television audiences

Decade	Television broadcast	Number of viewers
1950s	*Wagon Train* (western film), 1959	13 million
1960s	England v. Germany World Cup final, 1966	32 million
1970s	*Apollo 13* Moon astronauts return, 1970	28 million
1980s	*EastEnders*, 1986 Christmas episode	30 million
1990s	Princess Diana's funeral, 1997	32 million
2000s	*Only Fools and Horses* (comedy), 2001	21 million

Until 1955, Britain had only one television channel. More channels mean fewer occasions when everyone watches the same television programme.

Toys have also changed. In the 1950s, children played with puppets, train sets, model farms, clockwork cars, and board games. These toys are still around, but today over 70 per cent of children in Britain have a mobile phone and over 80 per cent have a games console. From 1950 (until it closed in 1970), one of Britain's most popular children's comics was *Eagle*, which had picture-story characters such as Dan Dare. Children still read books and comics, but also get a lot of their fun and information from television and the Internet.

Transformers have been popular toys since they were invented in 1984.

Pocket money

In 2008, a survey showed that the average child got over £6 a week pocket money. In 1987, it was about £1.

A survey asks questions. In this survey, 1,000 children aged 8 to 15 were asked about pocket money. Surveys provide useful information for historians, people who write about history.

Travel

In 1950, most people travelled by bus, bike, or train. A car ride was a treat, because few families had a car. Children went to the country or the seaside for summer holidays, usually by train. Very few children had ever been out of Britain.

Today, there are 15 times as many cars as in the 1950s. As more people bought cars, new roads were built. In 1959, Britain's first motorway (part of the London–Birmingham M1) was opened. More goods went by road, not rail, and so many small railway lines were closed. The last mainline steam train (a train pulled by a steam-driven locomotive) ran in 1968. In 1962, there were nearly 7,000 train stations; by 1970, there were fewer than 3,000.

More and more cars

1950	2 million
1970	10 million
1990	20 million
2007	27 million

This table shows how car ownership has grown since 1950.

In 1994, the first Eurostar trains sped through the Channel Tunnel between Britain and France. In 2007, a high-speed rail line linked the Tunnel to London.

In 1950, most planes were propeller-driven, and rather slow. Jet airliners like the Comet (see page 9) flew further and faster. By the 1970s, bigger "jumbo jets" like the Boeing 747 were landing every few minutes at London's Heathrow and other airports. The graph below shows how the number of air passengers is now 50 times greater than in the 1950s!

Most of the air travellers are holidaymakers, off to explore Europe, Australia, Asia, and the United States. Millions of foreign visitors also visit Britain every year. Tourism is now one of Britain's most important businesses.

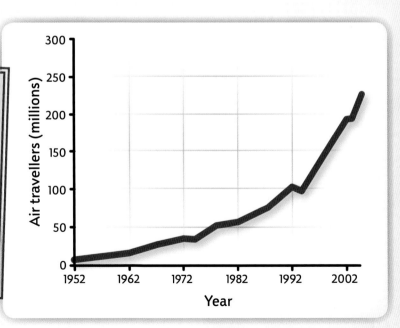

▲ These holidaymakers have travelled to the Spanish island of Majorca.

> Graphs are a visual (picture) way to show patterns or trends. The red line shows numbers at different points in time.

▲ This graph shows how the number of people using Britain's airports rose from less than 3 million in 1952 to 228 million in 2005.

United Kingdom?

Britain's position in the world has changed. In 1945, Britain was the centre of the **British Empire**. Over the next 30 years, almost all the countries Britain had ruled as **colonies** became independent. The Empire became the **Commonwealth**. Some new Commonwealth nations, such as India, Pakistan, and Nigeria, were much bigger than Britain. Others were small, such as St Kitts-Nevis in the Caribbean, or Fiji in the Pacific.

Britain is no longer one of the great powers, but it still plays a part in world affairs. British forces have been sent to Bosnia, Iraq, and Afghanistan, for example.

Many British people have family ties with Commonwealth nations, but since the 1970s Britain's laws and trade have been closely linked with Europe. The United Kingdom is one of 27 members of the **European Union** (EU). We still have our historic Parliament in London, but many of our laws are now made in the EU. Scotland, Wales, and Northern Ireland also make some of their own laws.

◀ This photograph shows Scotland's Parliament, where many laws affecting Scotland are now made.

Scotland's Parliament

In 1999, a Scottish Parliament met in Edinburgh, for the first time since 1707 (when England and Scotland were joined by the Act of Union). Scotland has a separate government and makes some of its own laws. Scottish Nationalists would prefer Scotland to be a completely independent nation.

Britain then and now

Facts and figures, like those in this book, help us see how history is made. To unlock the secrets of history we can look at **sources**. A source might be a letter, a photo, an old newspaper, or a diary. **Statistics**, for example how many more cars we have now, are useful too, especially in times of rapid change.

People live longer now. Today, **life expectancy** for a man is 76 years, and for a woman it is 80. In 1950, it was only 66 for men, and 71 for women. In Victorian times, in 1850, life expectancy was around 40 years.

To bring history alive, it is good to hear first-hand stories. Ask your family what they remember about growing up. Look around you to see if you can spot how your area may have changed. Then you will be unlocking Britain's history for yourself.

London then and now

In 1185, the historian Richard of Devizes wrote this about London: "all sorts of men crowd here from every country". Most cities have a mix of people. Today, nearly one-third of Londoners are from black and ethnic minorities.

▼ Many shops serve a mixed local community.

AFRO CARIBBEAN, ASIAN GROCERS AND GREENGROCERS

RETAIL

Timeline

1945   World War II ends

1947   India and Pakistan become independent nations

1948   National Health Service is set up; Olympic Games take place in London

1951   Festival of Britain takes place

1952   King George VI dies

1953   Queen Elizabeth II's **coronation** takes place

1955   Commercial television (ITV) begins

1956   Britain opens the world's first atomic power station, at Calder Hall, in Cumbria

1957   The Common Market is founded

1963   The Beatles hit the music charts

1967   First colour television programmes in Britain appear

1969   US **astronauts** land on the Moon

1970   Voting age in Britain is lowered from 21 to 18

1971   Britain's money goes decimal; the first email is sent

1973   Britain joins the Common Market

1979   Margaret Thatcher is Britain's first woman prime minister

1982   Britain fights Argentina in the Falklands War

1991   People start using the Internet; Helen Sharman is the first Briton in space; British forces take part in the Gulf War

1994   Channel Tunnel links Britain and France by train

1998   Good Friday Agreement in Northern Ireland, after many years of conflict

1999   Scottish Parliament meets in Edinburgh

2001   British troops sent to Afghanistan

2003   British forces take part in the Iraq War

Glossary

astronaut person who travels in space

British Empire countries ruled by Britain

broadband fast Internet access through a phone network

cassette magnetic tape device for recording and playing speech and music

colony territory settled and ruled by people from another country

Commonwealth association of countries, most of which were once part of the British Empire

coronation crowning ceremony for a new king or queen

council house home to rent, built by local governments (councils)

decade period of 10 years

European Union group of 27 countries that have agreed to work together

evidence picture, writing, or someone's account, that tells us what things were like at a particular time

immigrants people who migrate (travel) from one country to settle in another

life expectancy length of time a person is expected to live

new town planned town built on land that was green fields

rationing government control of the sale of food, fuel, clothes, and other goods

source form of historical evidence, such as a piece of writing or a picture

statistics numerical facts, or the science of collecting and analysing data

strike action by workers, who stop working as part of a dispute with their employer

vinyl record black plastic disc used to record music

Find out more

Books

Britain Since 1948: Home Life, Neil Tonge (Wayland, 2008)

Britain Since 1948: Technology, Neil Champion (Wayland, 2008)

Britain Since WWII: Immigration, Colin Hynson (Franklin Watts, 2007)

Britain Since WWII: Media and Entertainment, Colin Hynson
   (Franklin Watts, 2007)

Websites

You can find information, games, and a timeline on this website about
20th century London:

http://www.museumoflondon.org.uk/English/Collections/
   OnlineResources/X20L/default.htm

This useful timeline provides lots of facts about the 20th century in Britain:
http://www.localhistories.org/20thtime.html

Places to visit

The Time Machine Museum
12 The Square
Bromyard
Herefordshire HR7 4BP
www.timemachineuk.com

V&A Museum of Childhood
Cambridge Heath Road
London E2 9PA
www.vam.co.uk/moc

Index